Sh
Lost

Story by Betty Erickson
Illustrations by Kristine Dillard

Sherman went to school.
He looked in the gym,
but he didn't see Brad.
So Sherman went to look for him.

Sherman ran down the hall and stopped at the lost and found box.

Then Sherman looked in the library, but he didn't see Brad. Sherman liked stories. So he stayed to listen until he heard...

4

"Run, run, as fast as you can!" Sherman ran around the library until he heard...

5

"Stop, Gingerbread Man!"
Sherman stopped. Then he ran down
the hall to look for Brad again.

Next Sherman looked in the music
room, but he didn't see Brad.
Sherman liked music,
so he stayed to listen.

But Sherman didn't stay long.
He went to look for Brad.
Sherman stopped at the lost
and found box again.

And that's when Mr. Forest
saw Sherman.
"Out," he said.

9

Just then the bell rang, and
Miss Green came out of her office.
"Are you lost Sherman?" she said.

Then the teachers came down the hall
and said, "I lost my soccer ball."
"I lost my puppet."
"And I lost my maraca."

And Brad said,
"But my dog, Sherman,
found me!"